VOL. 7

HAL•LEONARD® KEYBOARD PLAY•ALONG

ROCK Classics

T0081544

CONTENTS

ISBN-13: 978-1-4234-1797-2
ISBN-10: 1-4234-1797-6

Visit Hal Leonard Online at www.halleonard.com

HAL•LEONARD®
CORPORATION
7777 W. BLUEMOUND RD. P.O. BOX 13819
MILWAUKEE, WISCONSIN 53213

Baba O'Riley

Words and Music by
Peter Townshend

Moderately (♩ = 120)

Play 11 times

Play 6 times

Play 7 times

*Sequenced keyboard arranged for piano.

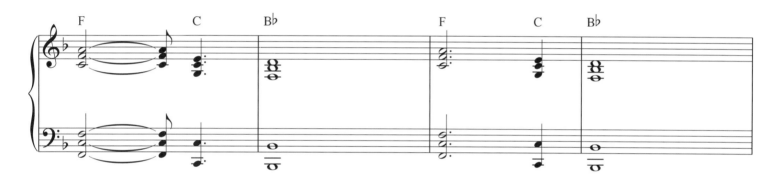

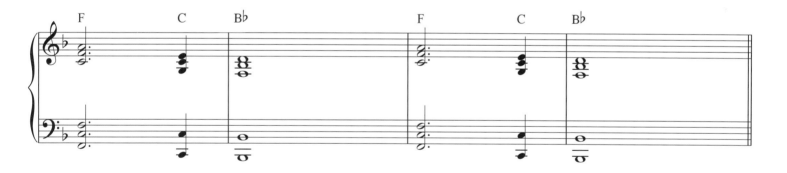

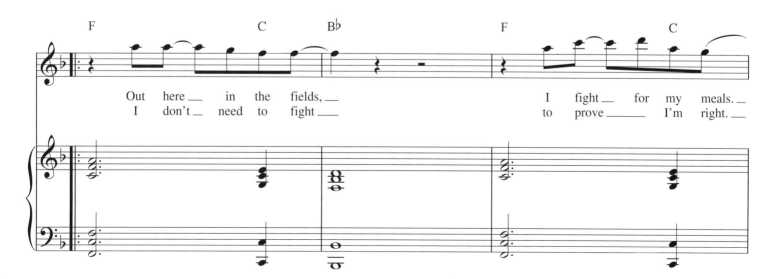

Out here ___ in the fields, ___   I fight ___ for my meals. ___
I don't ___ need to fight ___   to prove _____ I'm right. ___

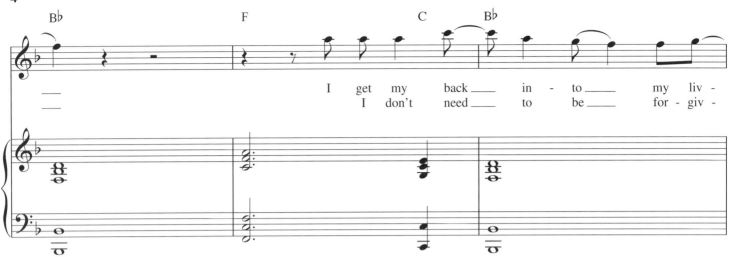

I get my back ___ in - to ___ my liv-
I don't need ___ to be ___ for - giv-

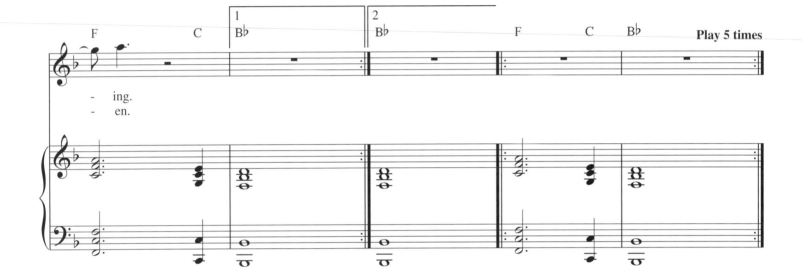

- ing.
- en.

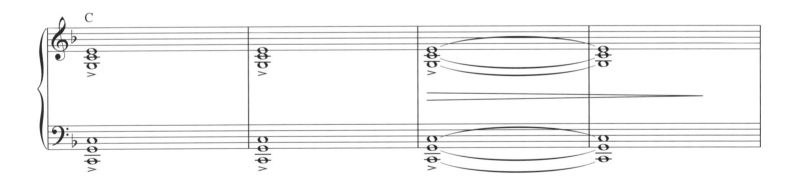

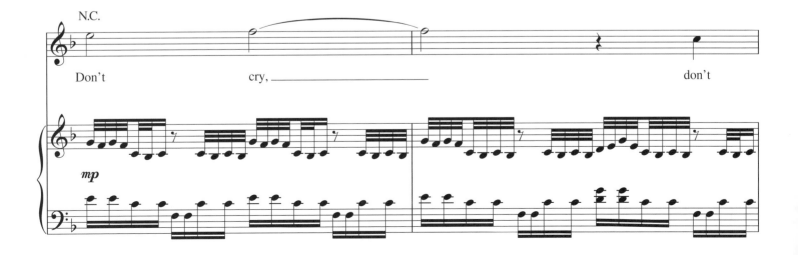

Don't   cry, _____   don't

raise   your   eye, _____   it's

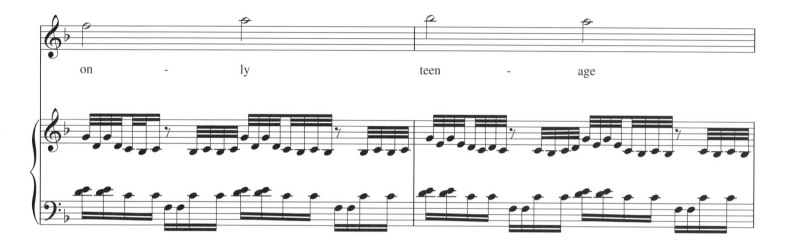

on - ly   teen - age

waste - land. _____

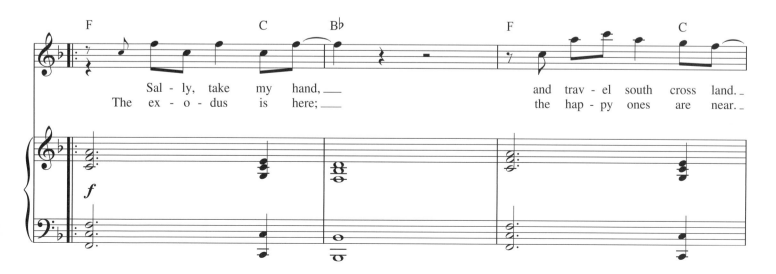

Sal - ly, take my hand, ___   and trav - el south cross land. __
The ex - o - dus is here; ___   the hap - py ones are near. __

F   C   B♭   F   C

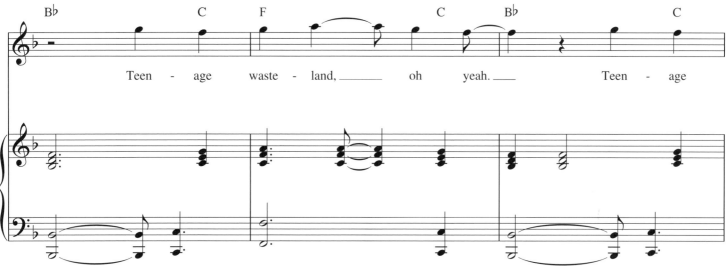

Teen - age waste - land, _____ oh yeah. _____ Teen - age

Faster ♩=172

waste - land.   They're all   wast - ed!

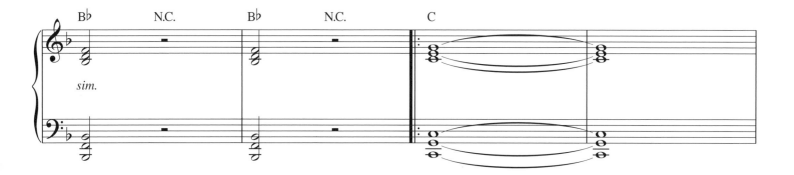

sim.

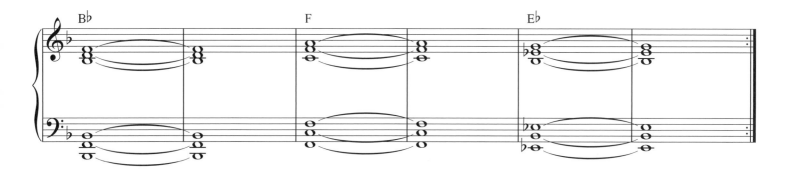

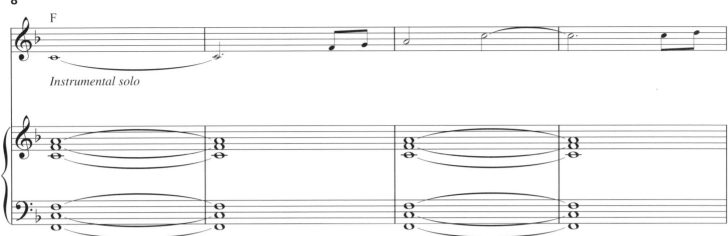

Instrumental solo

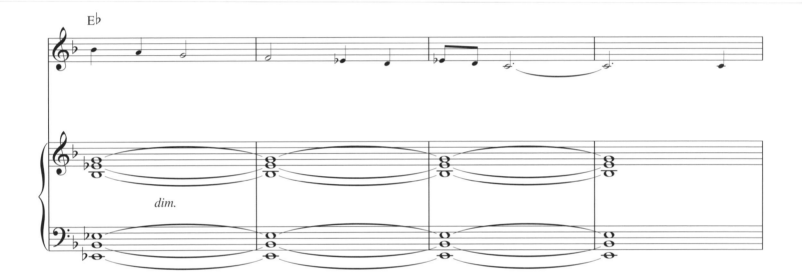

dim.

p

cresc. poco a poco

Bass

(Piano)

(Instrumental solo continues)

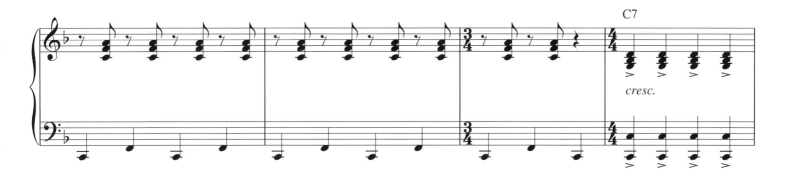

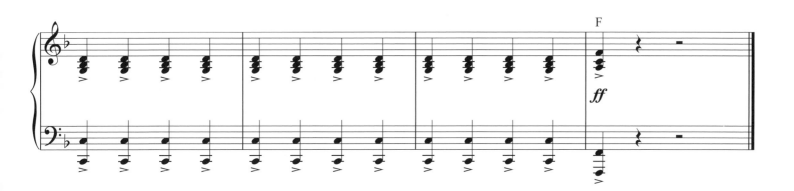

Bloody Well Right

Words and Music by Rick Davies
and Roger Hodgson

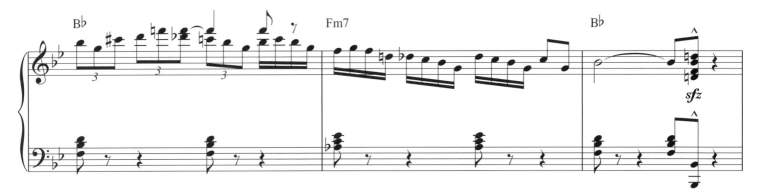

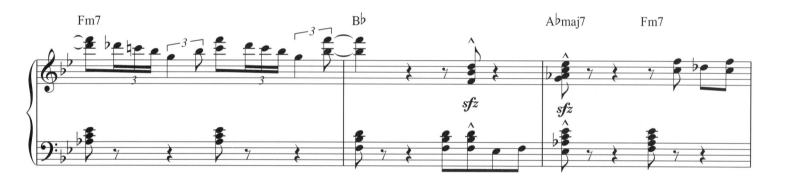

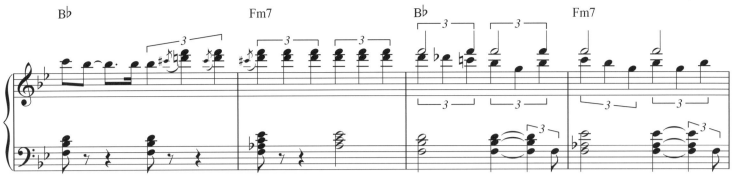

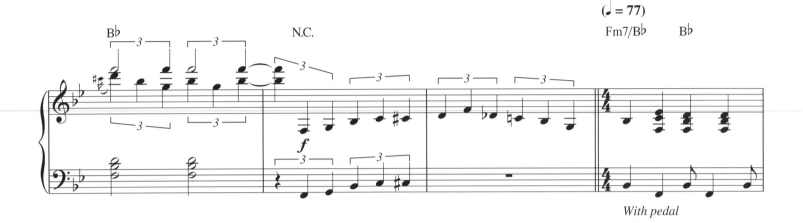

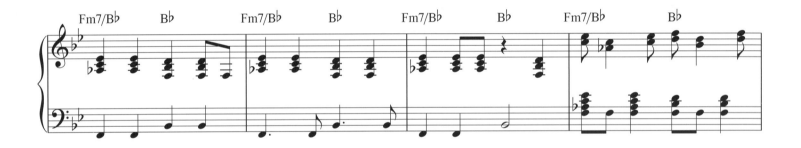

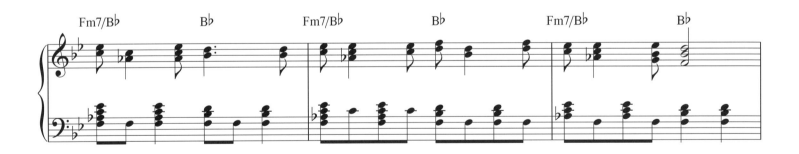

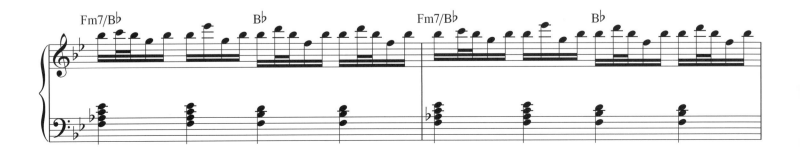

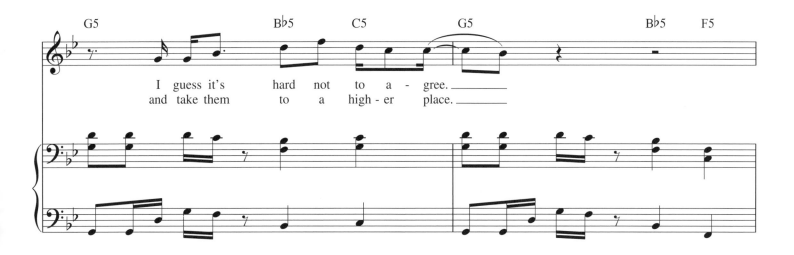

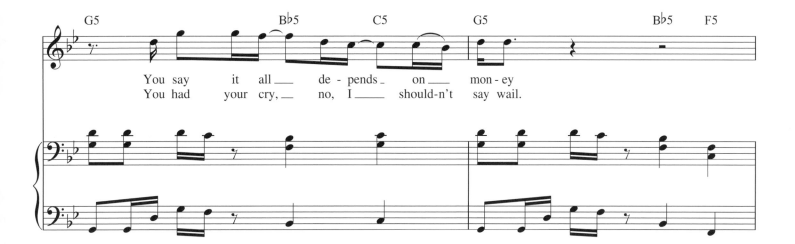

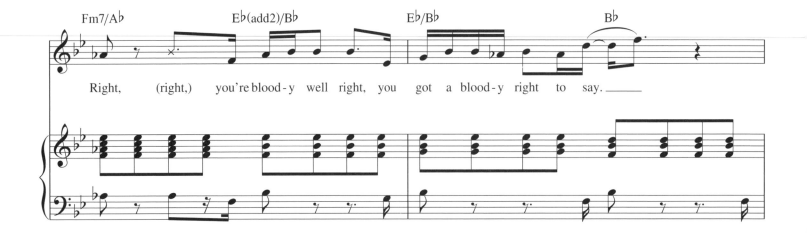

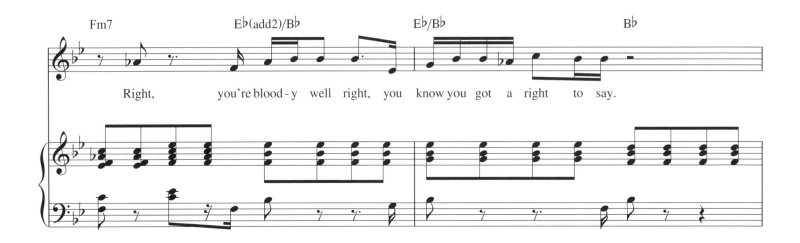

Yeah, yeah, you're blood-y well _ right, _ you know you're right to say, _ and
Yeah, yeah, you're blood-y well right, you know you got a right to say. _

me I don't care an-y-way.

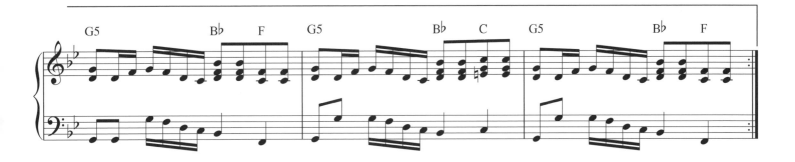

You got a blood-y right to say. _____

Repeat and Fade

Carry On Wayward Son

Words and Music by
Kerry Livgren

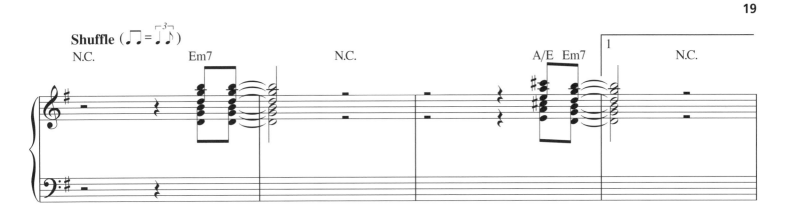

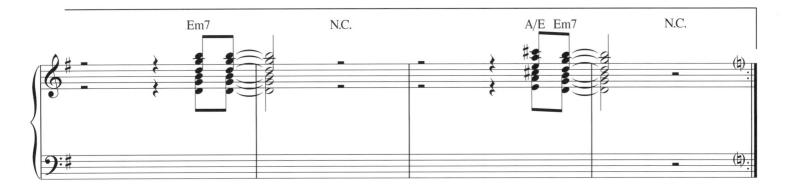

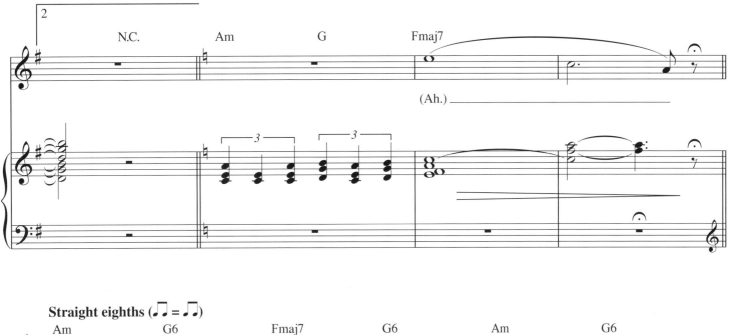

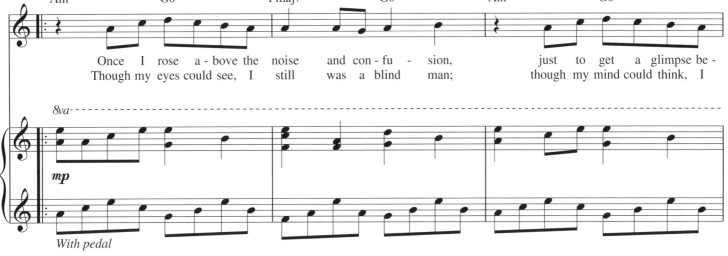

Once I rose a - bove the noise and con - fu - sion, just to get a glimpse be -
Though my eyes could see, I still was a blind man; though my mind could think, I

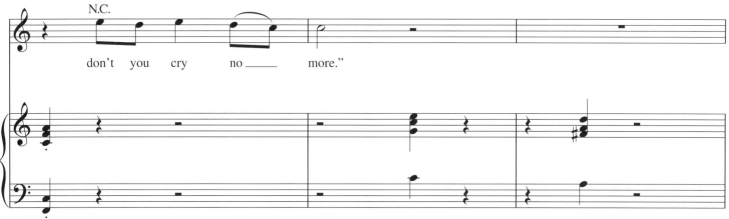

don't you cry no _____ more."

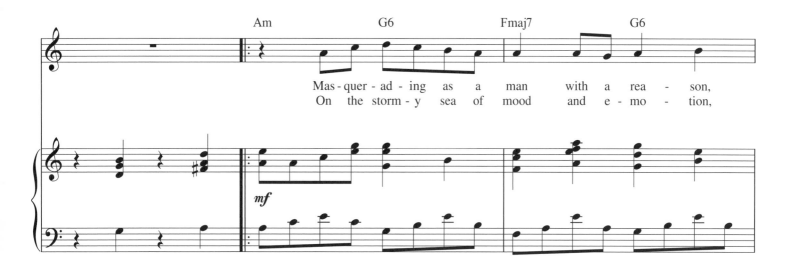

Mas - quer - ad - ing as a man with a rea - son,
On the storm - y sea of mood and e - mo - tion,

_mf_

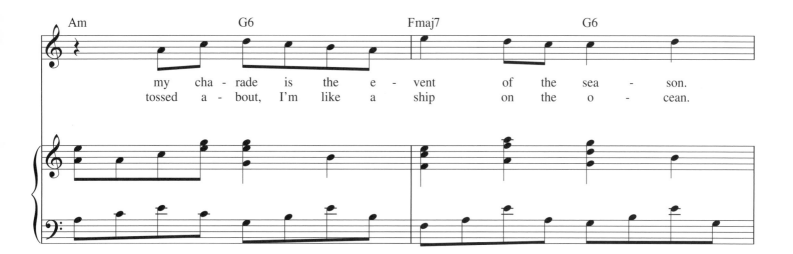

my cha - rade is the e - vent of the sea - son.
tossed a - bout, I'm like a ship on the o - cean.

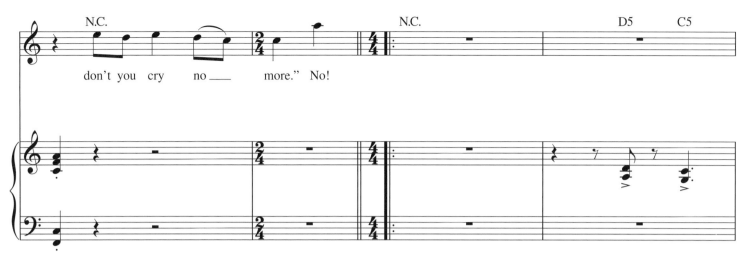

don't you cry no ___ more." No!

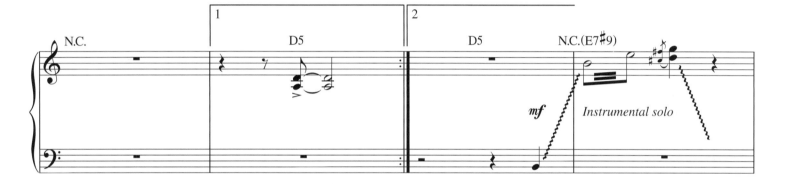

Solo ends

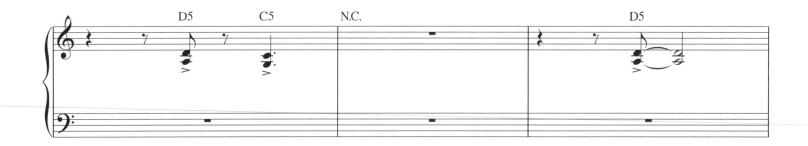

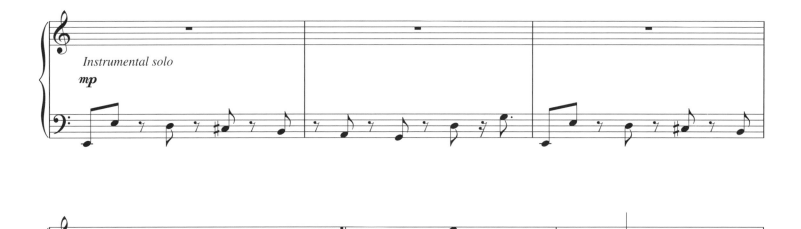

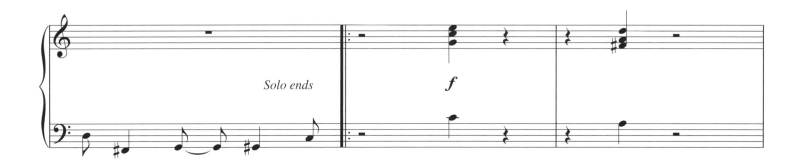

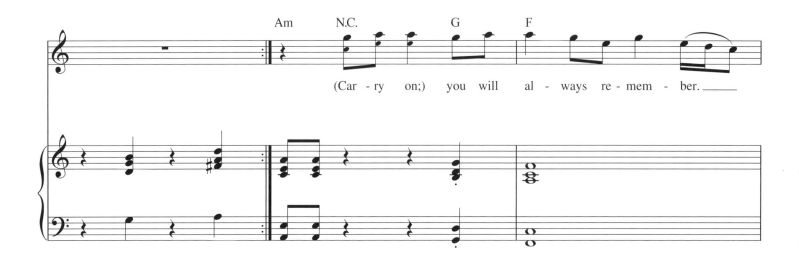

(Car - ry on;) you will al - ways re - mem - ber.

(Car - ry on;) none can e - qual the splen - dor. _____ Now your life's _ no long - er

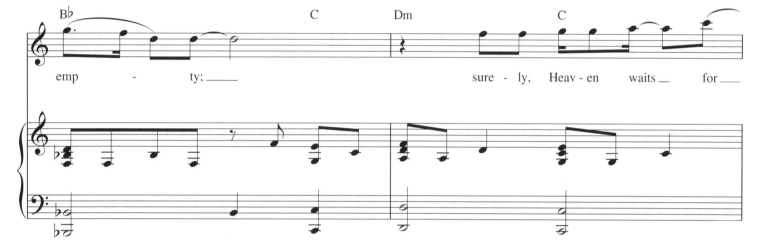

emp - - ty; _____ sure - ly, Heav - en waits _ for _

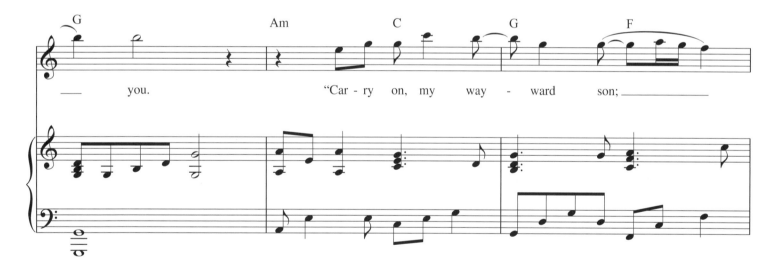

_ you. "Car - ry on, my way - ward son; _____

there'll be peace when you _ are done. _ Lay your wea - ry head _

to rest; _____ Don't you cry no

(don't you cry...) _____

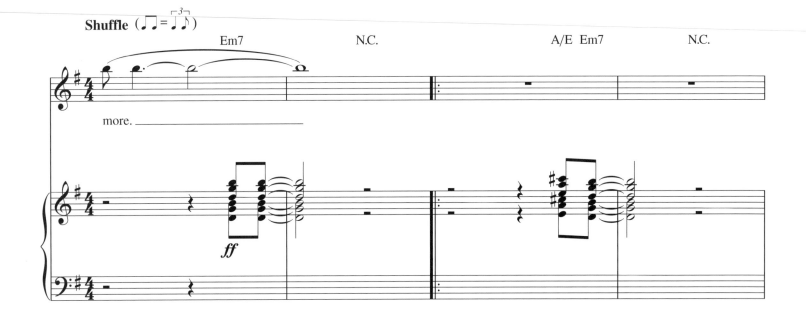

more. _____

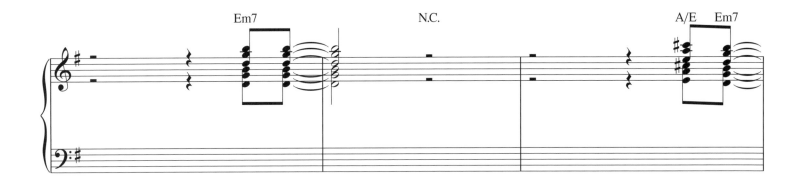

No   more! __

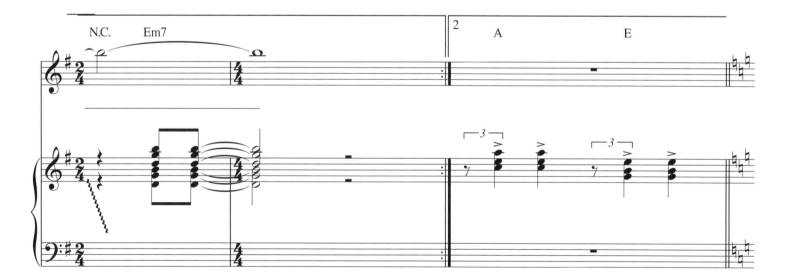

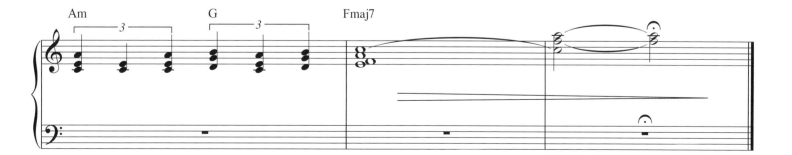

Changes

Words and Music by
David Bowie

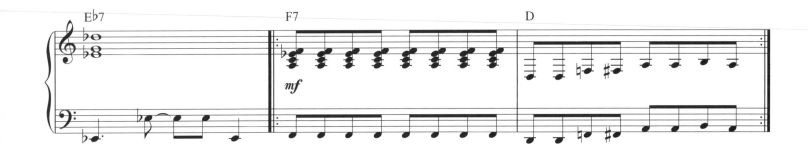

Still don't know what I ___ was wait - ing for ___ and my
I watch the rip - ples change their size ___ but

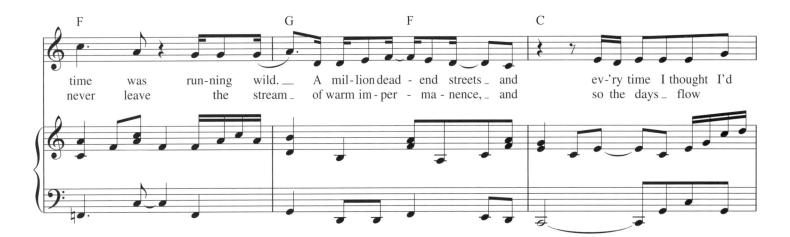

time was run - ning wild. ___ A mil-lion dead - end streets ___ and ev'-ry time I thought I'd
never leave the stream ___ of warm im-per - ma - nence, ___ and so the days ___ flow

got it made _ it seemed the taste was not so sweet. _ So I
through my eyes, _ but still the days seem the same. _ And these

turned _ my - self _ to face _ me, _ but I've nev-er caught a glimpse
chil - dren that you _ spit on as they try to change their worlds

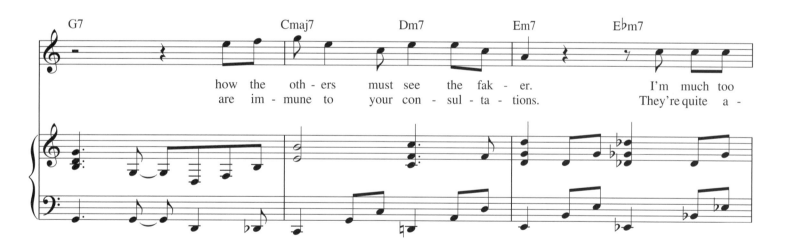

how the oth-ers must see the fak-er. I'm much too
are im-mune to your con-sul - ta-tions. They're quite a -

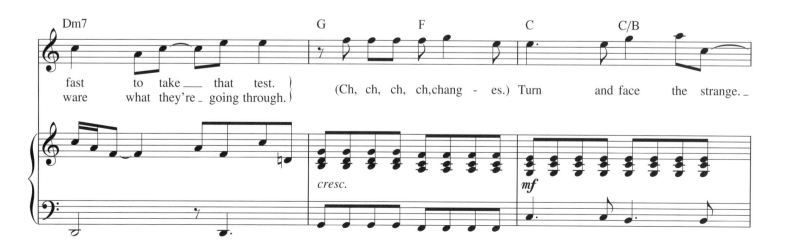

fast to take _ that test. }
ware what they're _ going through. } (Ch, ch, ch, ch,chang - es.) Turn and face the strange. _

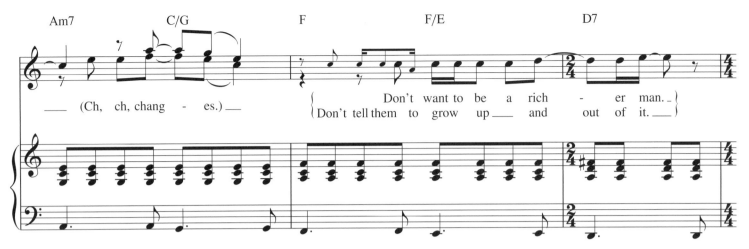

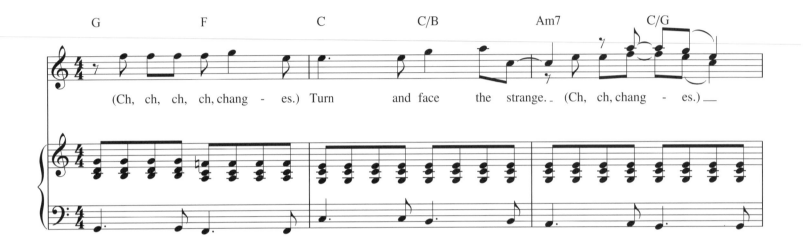

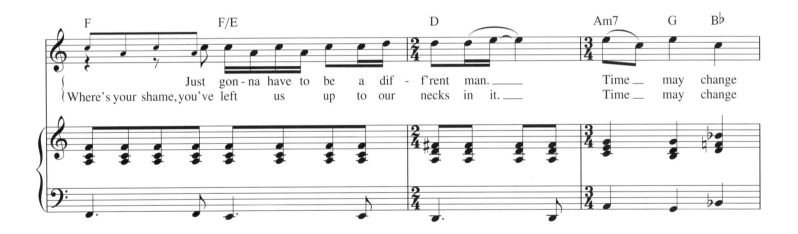

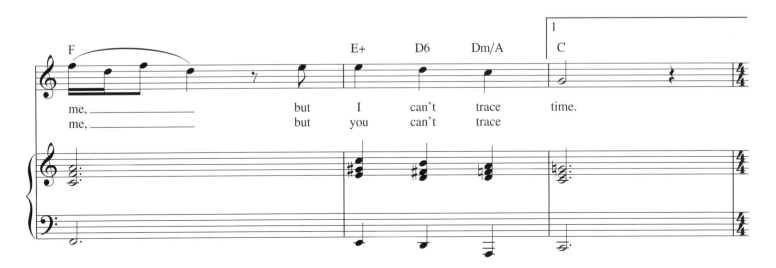

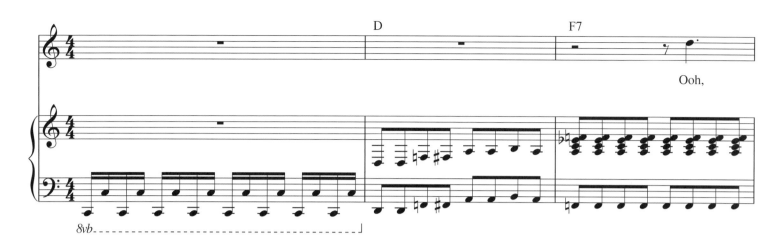

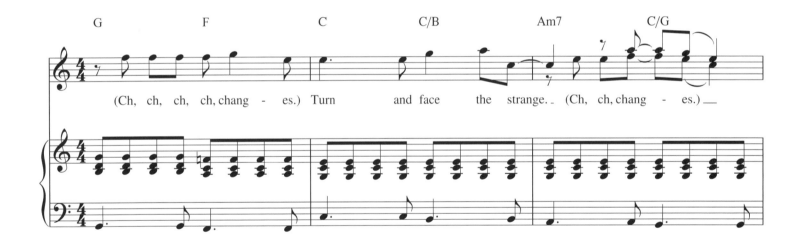

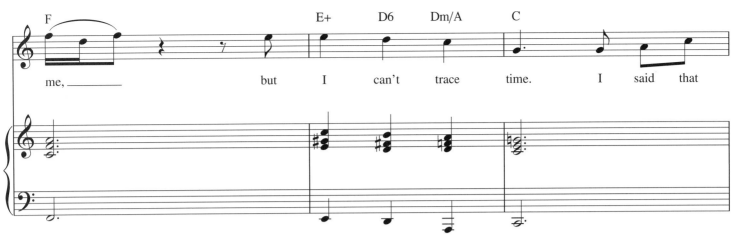

me, _____ but I can't trace time. I said that

time _____ may change me, _____ but I can't trace

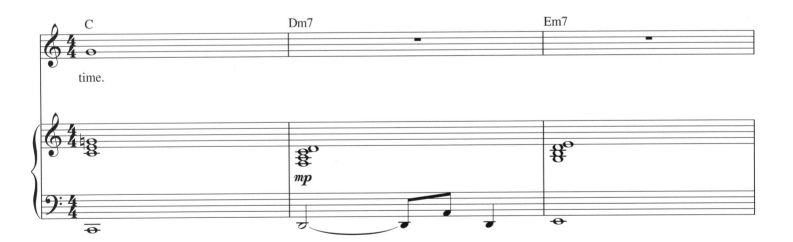

time.

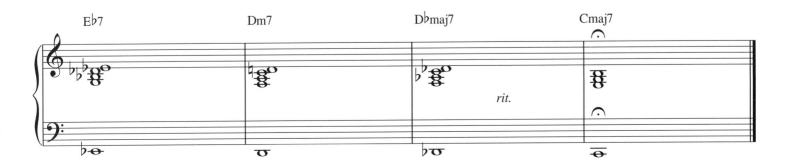

Cold as Ice

Words and Music by Mick Jones
and Lou Gramm

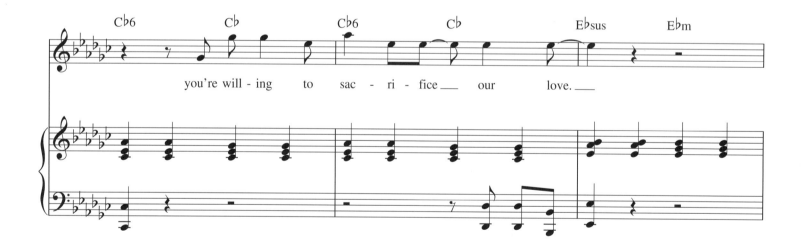

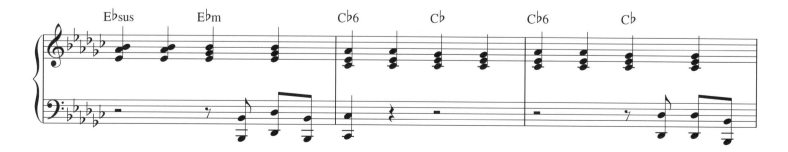

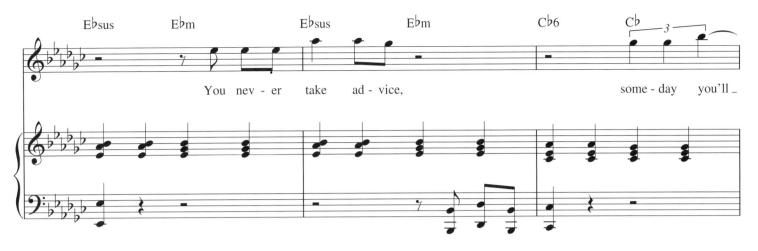

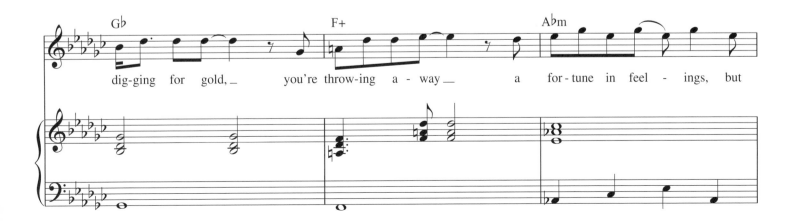

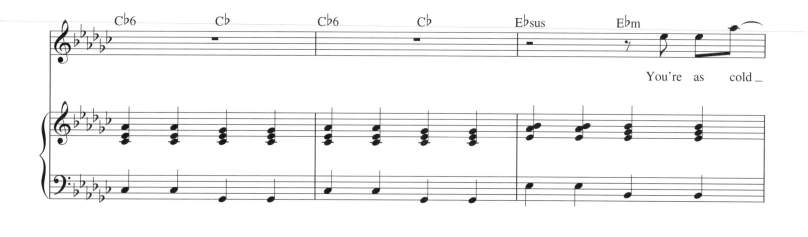

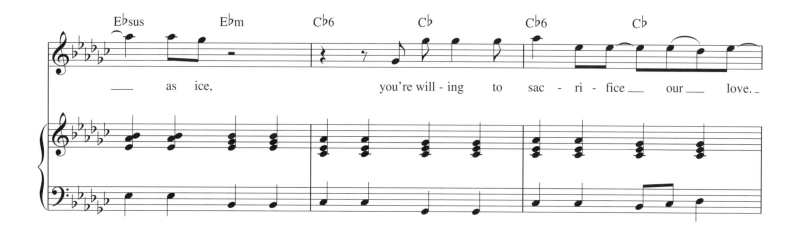

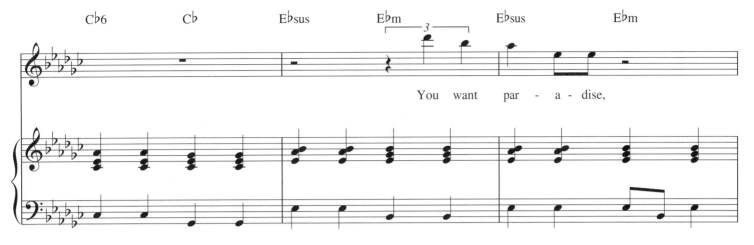

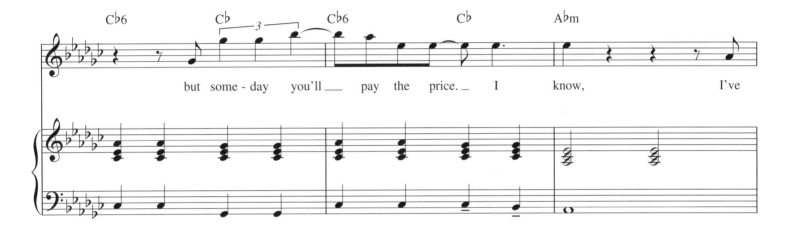

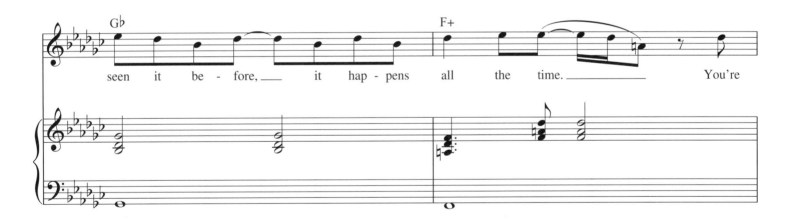

throw-ing a - way __ a for-tune in feel - ings __ must some-day you'll pay. __

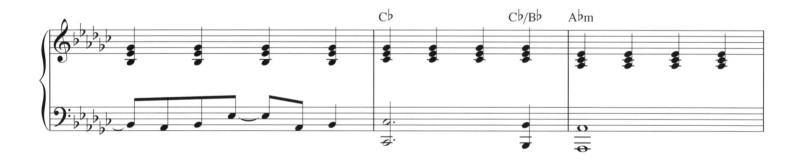

(Cold

With pedal

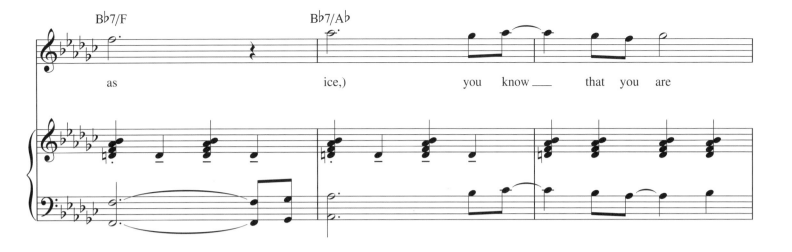

as ice,) you know ___ that you are

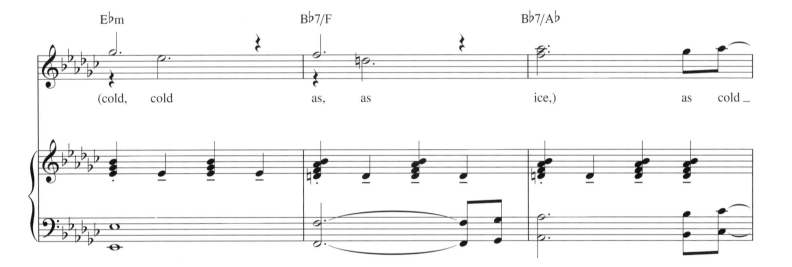

(cold, cold as, as ice,) as cold ___

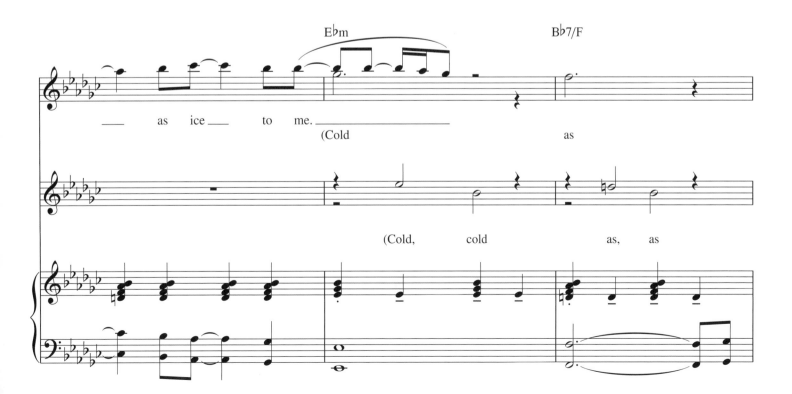

___ as ice ___ to me. (Cold as

(Cold, cold as, as

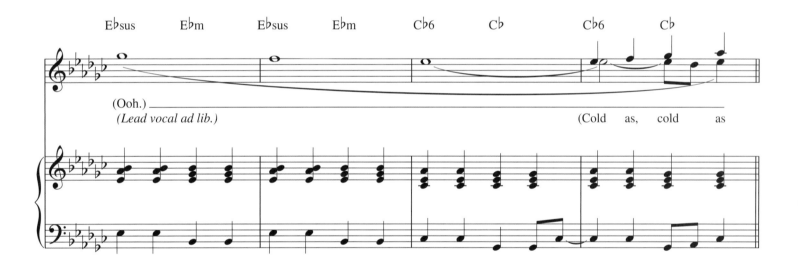

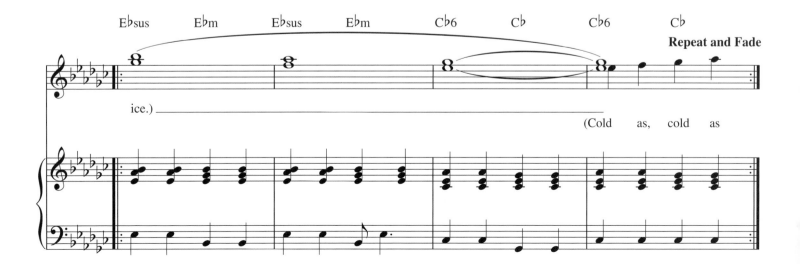

Evil Woman

Words and Music by
Jeff Lynne

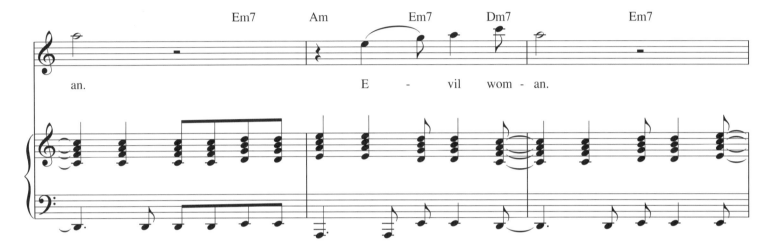

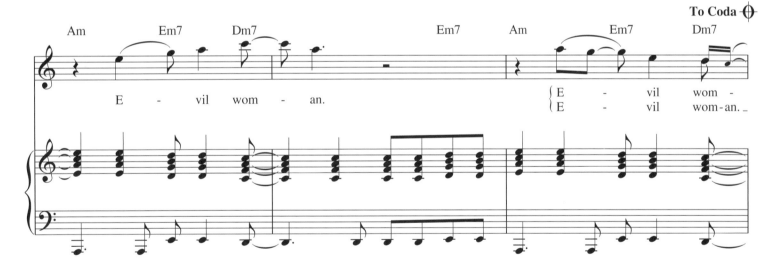

gold too hard to set - tle down. _ But a fool and his mon - ey soon go _

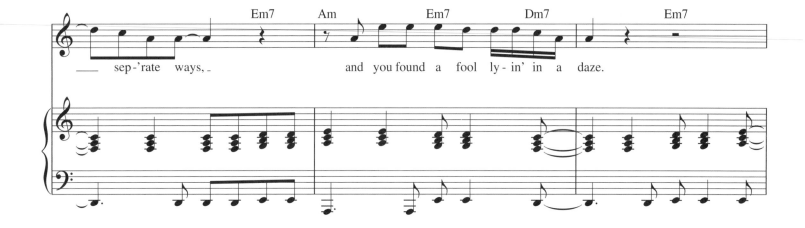

_ sep-'rate ways, _ and you found a fool ly - in' in a daze.

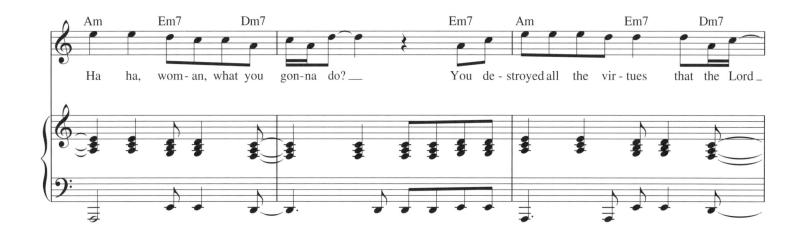

Ha ha, wom - an, what you gon-na do? _ You de - stroyed all the vir - tues that the Lord _

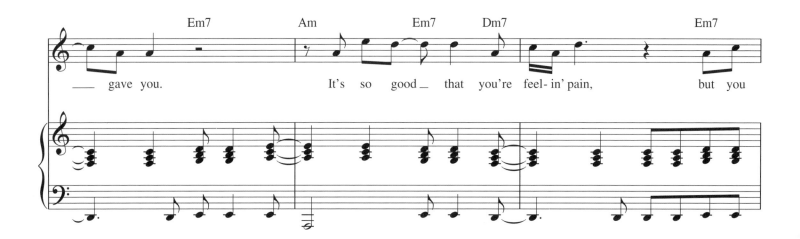

_ gave you. It's so good _ that you're feel - in' pain, but you

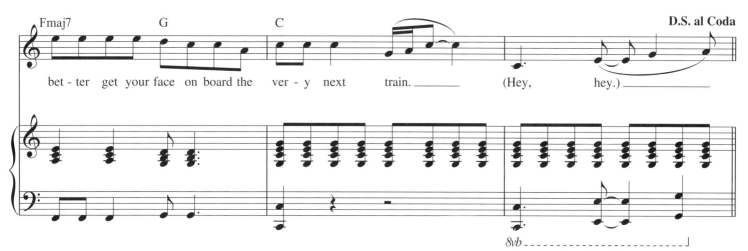

bet - ter get your face on board the ver - y next train._____ (Hey, hey.)_____

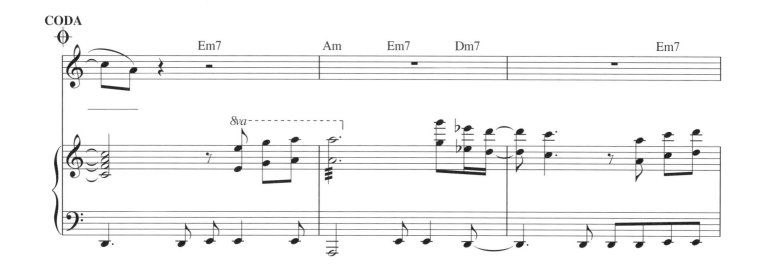

CODA

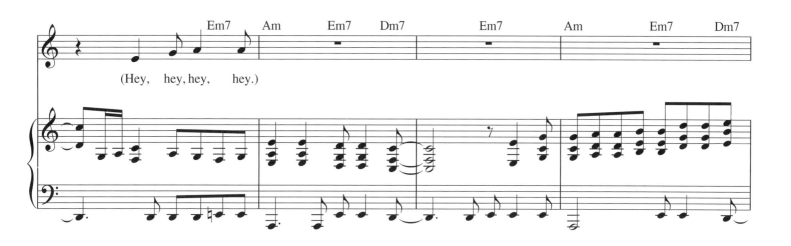

(Hey, hey, hey, hey.)

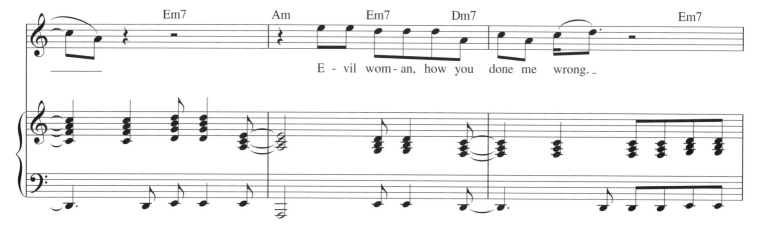

E - vil wom - an, how you done me wrong.

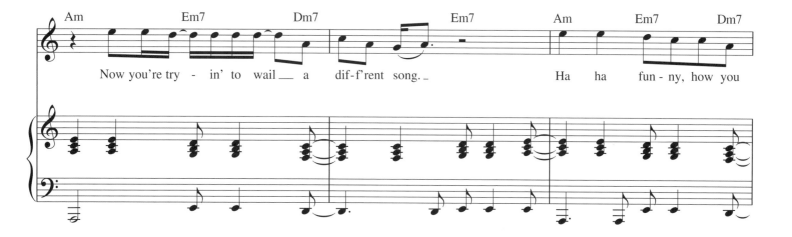

Now you're try - in' to wail __ a dif-f'rent song. __ Ha ha fun - ny, how you

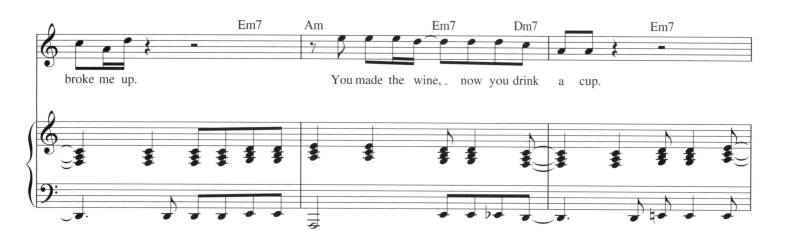

broke me up. You made the wine, __ now you drink a cup.

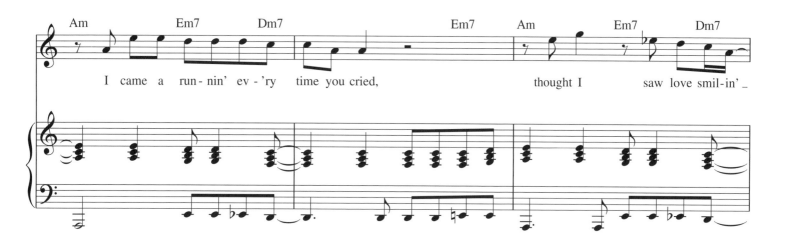

I came a run - nin' ev - 'ry time you cried, thought I saw love smil-in' __

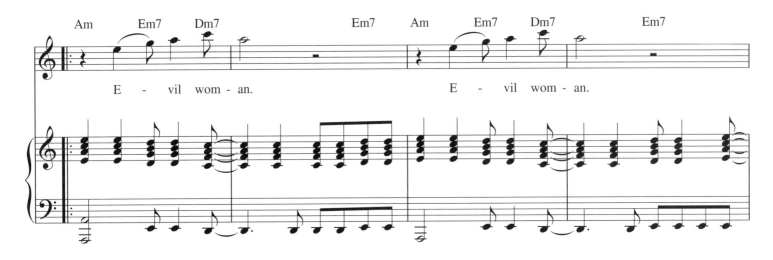

Space Truckin'

Words and Music by Ritchie Blackmore, Ian Gillan,
Roger Glover, Jon Lord and Ian Paice

They got mu-sic in their so-lar sys-tem; _____ they've

rocked a-round the Milk-y Way, _____ hey, hey, _____ hey. They dance a-round the Bo - re-al -

- ice; _____ they're space truck-in' ev-'ry day." _____

Come on! _____ Come

on!   Come on!   Let's   go   space truck- in'.   Come

(8vb)

on!   Come on!   Come on!

(8vb)

Space truck - in'.

Instrumental solo

(8vb)

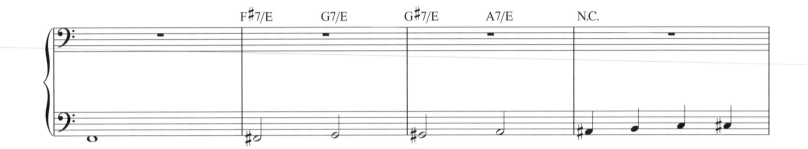

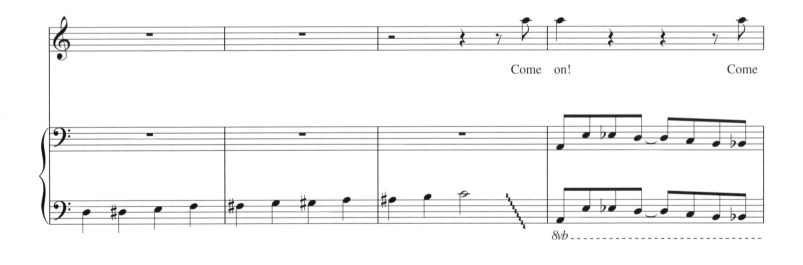

on!   Come   on!   Come   on!

Space   truck - in'.   Yeah,   yeah, —   yeah, —————— space   truck - in'.

Yeah,   yeah, —   yeah, —————— space   truck - in'.   Yeah,   yeah, —   yeah, ———

Repeat and Fade

—   space   truck - in'.   Yeah,   yeah, —   yeah, ——————— yeah,   yeah, yeah.

That's All

Words and Music by Tony Banks,
Phil Collins and Mike Rutherford

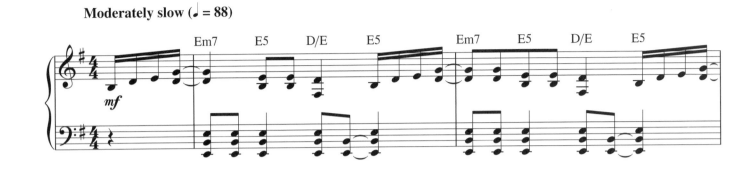

and you'd say __ night. Tell me it's black __ when I know that it's white. Al-ways the same, __

__ it's just a shame, and that's all. I could

leave but I __ won't go, though __ my heart might tell me so. __ I can't

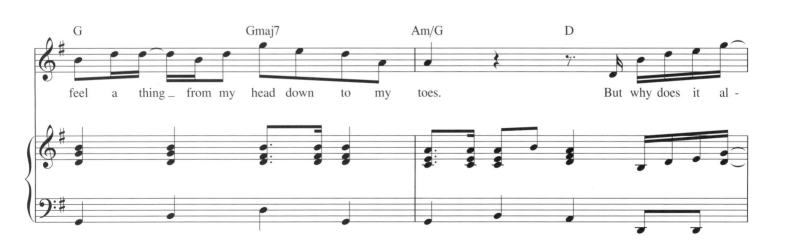

feel a thing __ from my head down to my toes. But why does it al -

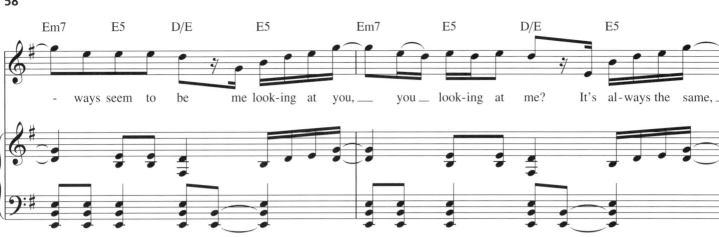

- ways seem to be me look-ing at you, __ you __ look-ing at me? It's al-ways the same, __

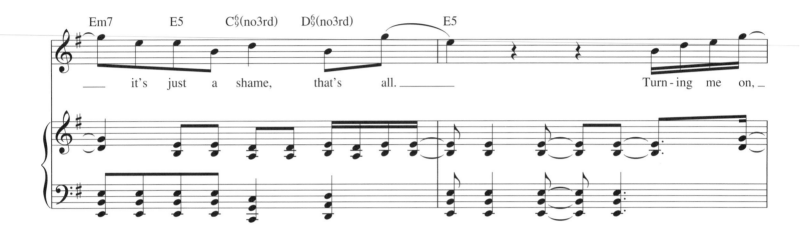

__ it's just a shame, that's all. _____ Turn-ing me on, __

__ turn-ing me off. Mak-ing me feel __ like I want too much. Liv-ing with you's

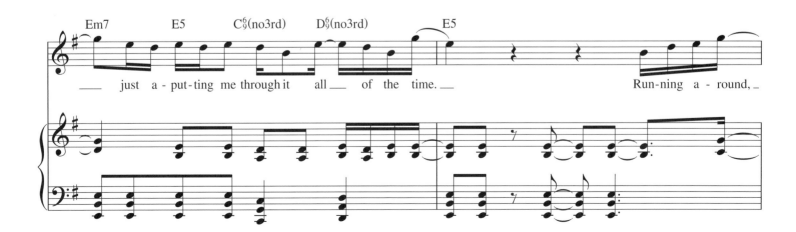

__ just a - put-ting me through it all __ of the time. __ Run-ning a - round,

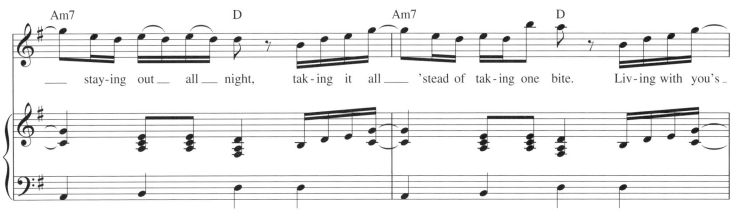

staying out all night, tak-ing it all 'stead of tak-ing one bite. Liv-ing with you's

just a-put-ting me through it all of the time. But I could

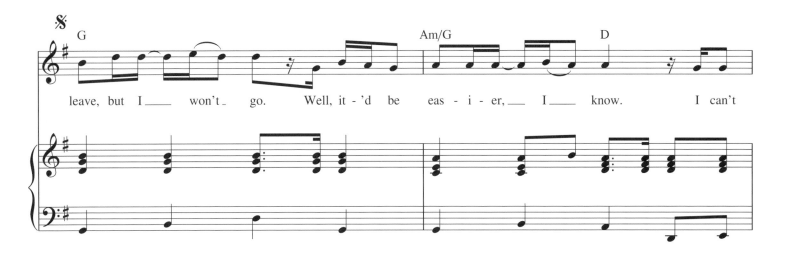

leave, but I won't go. Well, it-'d be eas-i-er, I know. I can't

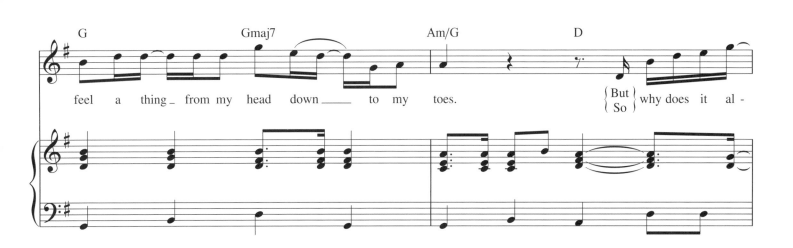

feel a thing from my head down to my toes. { But } { So } why does it al-

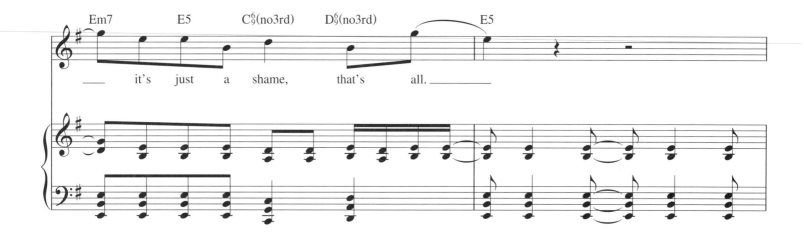

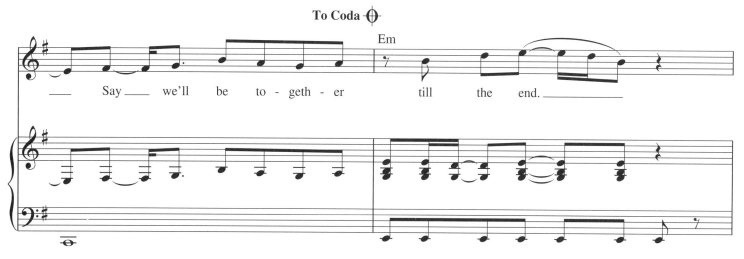

To Coda ⊕

Say we'll be to - geth - er till the end.

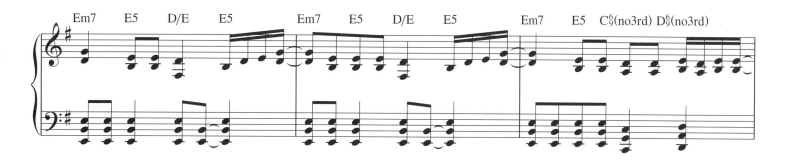

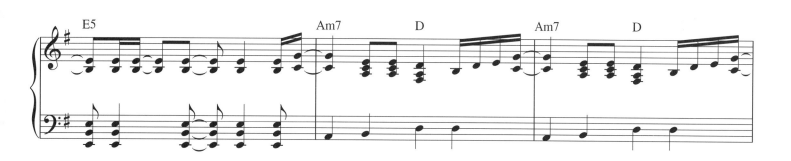

D.S. al Coda

But I could

CODA

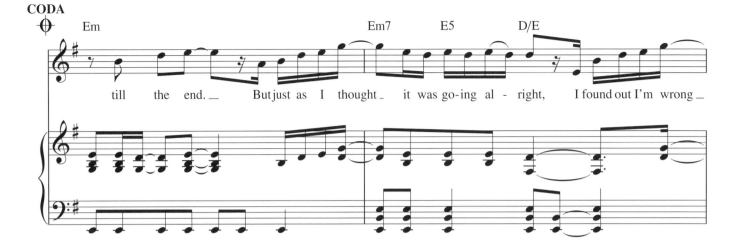

till the end. _ But just as I thought _ it was go-ing al - right, I found out I'm wrong _

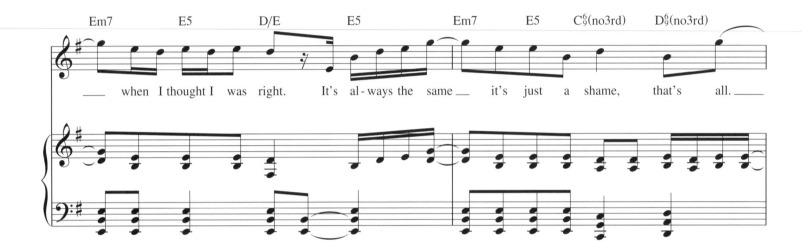

_ when I thought I was right. It's al - ways the same _ it's just a shame, that's all. _

_ Well, I could say day _ and you'd say night. Tell me it's black _

_ when I know that it's white. It's al - ways the same, _ it's just a shame, that's all. _

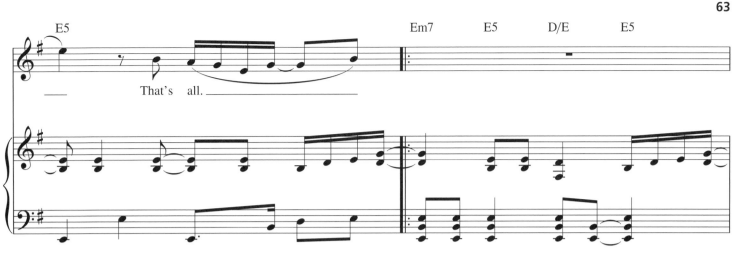

That's all.

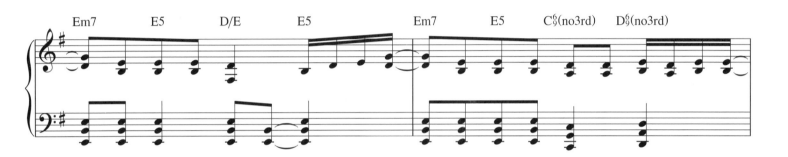

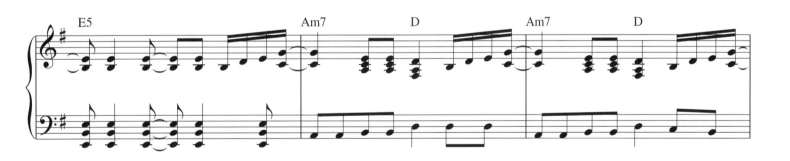

HAL·LEONARD KEYBOARD PLAY·ALONG

The Keyboard Play-Along series will help you quickly and easily play your favorite songs as played by your favorite artists. Just follow the music in the book, listen to the CD to hear how the keyboard should sound, and then play along using the separate backing tracks. The melody and lyrics are also included in the book in case you want to sing, or simply to help you follow along. The audio CD is playable on any CD player. For PC and Mac users, the CD is enhanced so you can adjust the recording to any tempo without changing pitch! Each book/CD pack in this series features eight great songs.

1. POP/ROCK HITS

Against All Odds (Take a Look at Me Now) (Phil Collins) • Deacon Blues (Steely Dan) • (Everything I Do) I Do It for You (Bryan Adams) • Hard to Say I'm Sorry (Chicago) • Kiss on My List (Hall & Oates) • My Life (Billy Joel) • Walking in Memphis (Marc Cohn) • What a Fool Believes (The Doobie Brothers).
00699875 Keyboard Transcriptions...$14.95

2. SOFT ROCK

Don't Know Much (Aaron Neville) • Glory of Love (Peter Cetera) • I Write the Songs (Barry Manilow) • It's Too Late (Carole King) • Just Once (James Ingram) • Making Love Out of Nothing at All (Air Supply) • We've Only Just Begun (Carpenters) • You Are the Sunshine of My Life (Stevie Wonder).
00699876 Keyboard Transcriptions...$12.95

3. CLASSIC ROCK

Against the Wind (Bob Seger) • Come Sail Away (Styx) • Don't Do Me like That (Tom Petty and the Heartbreakers) • Jessica (Allman Brothers) • Say You Love Me (Fleetwood Mac) • Takin' Care of Business (Bachman-Turner Overdrive) • Werewolves of London (Warren Zevon) • You're My Best Friend (Queen).
00699877 Keyboard Transcriptions...$14.95

4. CONTEMPORARY ROCK

Angel (Sarah McLachlan) • Beautiful (Christina Aguilera) • Because of You (Kelly Clarkson) • Don't Know Why (Norah Jones) • Fallin' (Alicia Keys) • Listen to Your Heart (D.H.T.) • A Thousand Miles (Vanessa Carlton) • Unfaithful (Rihanna).
00699878 Keyboard Transcriptions...$12.95

5. ROCK HITS

Back at One (Brian McKnight) • Brick (Ben Folds) • Clocks (Coldplay) • Drops of Jupiter (Tell Me) (Train) • Home (Michael Buble) • 100 Years (Five for Fighting) • This Love (Maroon 5) • You're Beautiful (James Blunt)
00699879 Keyboard Transcriptions...$14.95

6. ROCK BALLADS

Bridge over Troubled Water (Simon & Garfunkel) • Easy (Commodores) • Hey Jude (Beatles) • Imagine (John Lennon) • Maybe I'm Amazed (Paul McCartney) • A Whiter Shade of Pale (Procol Harum) • You Are So Beautiful (Joe Cocker) • Your Song (Elton John).
00699880 Keyboard Transcriptions...$14.95

More Volumes Coming Soon, Including:
Vol. 7 Rock Classics

Prices, contents, and availability subject to change without notice.

FOR MORE INFORMATION,
SEE YOUR LOCAL MUSIC DEALER,
OR WRITE TO:

HAL·LEONARD®
CORPORATION
7777 W. BLUEMOUND RD. P.O. BOX 13819
MILWAUKEE, WISCONSIN 53213

Visit Hal Leonard Online at **www.halleonard.com**

0707